Atlantic International University
A New Age for Distance Learning

ROBERT D. BENDA

ID #: UM32356BPR40930

INTERNATIONAL PROJECT MANAGEMENT

INTERNATIONAL PROJECT MANAGEMENT: THE DECISIVE TOOL FOR INTERNATIONAL DEVELOPMENT PROJECTS IN DEVELOPING COUNTRIES.

ATLANTIC INTERNATIONAL UNIVERSITY
HONOLULU, HAWAII

NOVEMBER 2014

TABLE OF CONTENTS

i

1.0 INTRODUCTION

International project management is fundamental to the success of international development projects, but their poor implementation and management strategy can result to little or no outcomes or desired results. With my attention on international project management as a tool for impact in international development projects, I analyze in this paper, international project management, its relationship and impact to international development projects in developing countries.

The contribution of this paper is aimed at making international development projects more efficient, effective, and as such it proposes a number of ways in which

1

international project management could be used as a decisive tool to support a precise and unique implementation strategy of international development projects successfully to yield results. It also could be of great assistance to good project management practices as it looks at projects and project management in the precise and evolving area of the increasing purview of project management – to be specific international development projects. This paper further discusses, proposes and outlines four (4) project management strategies or concepts to practice in the implementation of international development projects to achieve project goals and results. These suggested strategies, when proficiently practiced to can bring to conclusion, the failure of many international development projects in developing countries,

and contribute potentially to international project management as regards international development projects.

2.0 DESCRIPTION

The idea of international development projects began some years back by project management establishments designing guidelines and procedures for achieving impact in development projects. The main concern of these project management institutions was focused on the design/formulation of project management techniques be employed by implementing agencies/project managers to meet the growing demands/needs of international development projects as many of them were not successfully implemented.

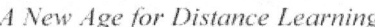 
Agencies that provide funding to implementing agencies for the implementation/management of international development projects are more focused on the impact of projects and not their ineffectiveness and failure. All of these international development projects are geared towards and using project management techniques to turn things around positively in the management/implementation of projects towards achieving desirable outcomes/goals and impact in developing countries.

If funding provided by donor agencies are not expended on development projects and there are no tangible result or no impact, it means that the projects can be branded as a failure. Development project are meant to be effective and efficient

when they are implemented and are supposed to yield anticipated outcomes as well.

I believe international development projects can still be part of the determinant factor in international development, provided it will be managed with the full awareness of specifically designed project management strategies as a necessity for implementing development projects. It is fundamentally good to note that the misapplication of international project management techniques generate serious management problems or even difficulties in the implementation of development projects in developing countries thus resulting to project failure-this ought to be cut

5

in partial or even totally if we must succeed in achieving desired project goals. In reality, the management practices of these projects and the indicator to determine whether international development projects are considered (successful or failed projects) can be predominantly be indicated by these developing countries' governmental economy system and the manner in which these projects are managed by their governmental representatives and implementing agencies. International development projects success or failure also can be characterized by the management process associated with its implementation.

The significance of international project management in the current program management approach, and the uncertain results of projects or whether they are financed by national

6

governments or international organizations, international project management is still relevant in international development projects. Unlike now where project management and international development are associated with the high growth of developments, it was the complete opposite in the last 5 decades because they were not aligned greatly to the ideas and knowledge of international development. International project management offers so many new techniques and skills in managing projects now a day more than it did in the 21st century. Today, project managers can acquire so much knowledge in the field of project management relating to managing projects at every stage of the project lie-cycle and this allows development projects to be implemented with much more success as we

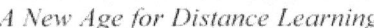

speak. Again, we can adopt the international project management strategies I will propose in this paper as a tool for international development all over the world in a bid to reverse ineffectiveness of international development projects in the past when they were implemented with outcomes and goals not achieved and impact not felt due to poor project management. I believe that, with advanced project management techniques now available to project managers and teams, considerable progress can be made in managing international development projects efficiently and effectively considering the more recent contributions of international project management as a field of knowledge to international development.

3.0 GENERAL ANALYSIS

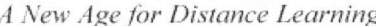

International Project Management strives to foster international networks for future employment, cooperation, and knowledge interchange and partnership arrangements. It also improves the capacity of project managers to work exceptionally in multicultural teams and manage variety and multiculturalism in the management of international development projects. International project management enables strategic change within vigorous internal and external organizational environs, with potential to increase worth economically and socially by formulating combined effect between parties.

Many international projects are sometimes implemented in several different frameworks to include: managerial, economic, and political. This is quite different from those

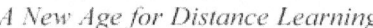

implemented in developed countries. Numerous international development projects are funded by international development agencies while others are funded by many other governmental and international nongovernmental organizations (INGOs). The purpose of these development projects is to improve the lives and livelihoods of under-privileged people in other parts of the world. These projects can range from small to super extra-large projects and can cover all sectors of development in countries around the world. They do have a start and end date and begin from the preparation stage to the implementation stage and on ward to the monitoring and evaluation stage. They can be implemented for the development, advancement and improvement of poor countries.

International development projects can depict capacity building, social development, economic advancement, governmental policies reform, and infrastructural changes in the life of very poor people as well as a specific purpose based on the size, location, and timeline of the project. These projects are aimed towards achieving common goals or contributing to the overall economic growth or poverty reduction program of the people in a country. They are usually funded for the purpose of achieving results and long term impact that will improve the lives and livelihoods of the targeted beneficiaries thereby contribution to the country's overall development agenda as in the case of the Poverty Reduction Strategy (PRS) in Liberia. Lastly, international development projects are, at the same time formulated with

concepts that are in response to perceived developmental situational necessities, income-generating activities, or investments with definite economic proceeds and sequences of activities (**Khang & Moe, 2008**).

4.0 ACTUALIZATION

We have read and seen before how international development projects are particularly specific in nature. As a result, the management methods of international development projects are also specific as well. Hence, a

precise approach of international project management prevails in international development projects, as its usage of project management approaches, tools, and techniques is specific. International development projects can usually be financed by donations, loans or grants, and the funding agency often leads the identification of these projects and the fortitude of their detailed objectives. International development projects are identified, organized/prepared, and implemented in a detailed and precise context. Under the current World Bank program approach, typical international development projects would be part of a program and fit well into a comprehensive development frameworks (**European Commission, 2007**).

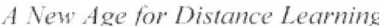

Stakeholders are very important and must be taken seriously in the implementation of international development projects because they play a very crucial role in the outcome of the project. Usually, stakeholders can be grouped into four (4) categories: the people that are directly affected, those that are indirectly affected; the government and public sector departments and funding agencies, project specialists, project managers, and entrepreneurs.

Again, we can generally say or agree that the unique environments in which international development projects are implemented make them very specific in nature as this depends on how the international development projects are characterized by project application techniques and activities and the relative intangibility of their ultimate objective of

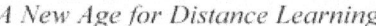

poverty reduction at a large assortment of heterogeneous stakeholders and the divergent perspectives among these stakeholders involved with the project implementation.

Certainly, none of these project management circumstances are essentially exceptional to international development projects and international project management. We read more and more about how complex projects in the standard project management are done and practiced with the experience of a number of these difficult circumstances surrounding their implementation considering whether they are local, national or international projects. However, these situations all together challenge the management process of contract-based precepts and procedure of standard project management with some of these practices inquiring whether

project management is an incongruity in the field of international development projects. It is also a collectively result in a specific set of problems facing project management in international development projects, which I will discuss in the next section of this paper (**Golini, et al, 2014**).

5.0 DISCUSSIONS

The World Bank and other funding agencies over the past few years have invested billions worth of dollars in hundreds international development projects in developing countries in the last two decades and the failure rate of these projects has been a little more than half of the total international

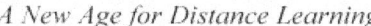
development projects implemented. This is largely due to the fact that the implementing agencies did not perform with much further success.

The misapplication of international project management tool and approaches has largely contributed to the failure of many international development projects in developing countries. In addition to the often heard complaints that developing countries are the toughest part of the world for implementing development projects and that those developing countries lack highly qualified people, I strongly suggest that international project management be practiced by project managers as the decisive tool in implementing international development projects in developing countries to achieve desired results. I will now turn to discussing achieving

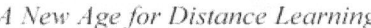

international development goals and objective using international development project management as a tool for international development projects in developing countries.

In the following paragraphs I outlined and discussed four (4) keys strategies (approaches) international project management approaches (tools) or procedures to practice in the implementation of international development projects in a bid to successfully achieve desirable project goals and objectives in developing countries.

5.1 Strategy #1: The Decisive Project Management Approach

I would define the decisive project management approach as a technique that is focused on achieving project objectives

and outcomes and resolves specific problems that are related to international development projects with a purpose of producing impact.

While it is true that a number of problems have affected the effective outcome of international development projects, the best tool to apply in resolving these problems for the attainment of development project goals and objectives is the practice of the decisive project management approach as a tool in managing development projects for results. International project management can be instrumental and in the implementation of international development project in developing countries by using it as a critical implementation device to institute amenable changes to virtually achieve the deliverables.

Here I suggest that international development project problems be dealt with using the decisive international project approach technique which aims to technically resolve the problems associated and responsible for the failure of international development projects in developing countries.

International development projects can largely benefits developing countries by the usage of the decisive project management approach in its management/implementation which includes having a proportional responsibility over the management of the time, resources, quality and costs of the project to have positive impacts on the local populations and the country at large.

5.2 Strategy #2: The Organizational Approach

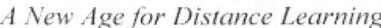

The organizational approach is a project management application technique that upholds the vision, mission and goal of the implementing agency (organization/institution) throughout the project implementation stage. International development projects are confronted with serious organizational challenges and remedy to resolving these difficulties can only be done through the organizational approach. This project management strategy has been proven over the years to be very effective in managing international development project with a goal to maintain the organization's goal and objectives. Nevertheless, a comprehensive awareness of the organizational approach can be a step forward in resolving the challenges associated with international development projects.

5.3 Strategy #3: The Concept of the Managerial Approach

International development projects frequently fail to achieve their outcomes and goals due to a number of problems that derive from poor management approaches or concepts. The miss-application of the managerial approach in development projects is a primary reason for the poor record of implementation of development projects in many developing countries. The inability of implementing agencies and project managers to effectively manage development projects continues to be a major obstacle to the development of the poorest of the poor societies. Despite the intensive experience with project investment, international funding institutions and agencies of less developed countries still report serious problems in project management and

execution. Many are due directly to ineffective planning and management.

Executing projects using the concept of the Managerial approach can play an extraordinary role in the success of international development projects. The fact that many of the problems that are found to cause project to fail brings into the picture the execution of the managerial approach which when used properly , can impact development projects massively and yield desirable deliverables and positive results. In the past, there was no good managerial supervision and coordination which led to the failure of these projects. The managerial approach when used effectively can tackle and resolve managerial problems related to project failures which are thus derived from: undefined objectives and insensitivity

23

of project supervisors and managers to address the needs of beneficiaries. It is also as a result of the non-existence of skilled project management personnel, who lack the requisite qualification to manage these projects. If an international development project is, first and foremost, a project, one could argue that utilizing the managerial approach to project management would offer useful methodologies, approaches, and tools and techniques for international development projects. The practice of the managerial approach points toward the potential usage and support of a critical method, which draws on broader critical discourses to embed management context in our understanding of the operation and impact of international project management on

international development projects in developing countries

(**Ahsan & Gunawan, 2010**).

5.4 Strategy #4: The Sustainable Approach Concept

While other problems may explain international development

project failures in developing countries, sustainability has

been one of the challenges associated with the failure of

international development projects. Sustainability has

triggered a lot of project to fail because implementing

agencies sometimes ignore this concept with insensitivity-not

knowing that the long term impact of any project lies within

its sustainability. The lack of sustainability in international

development projects can result to 'no long term project impact' which has the propensity to potentially increase the unfavorable condition as regards the effectiveness of international development projects, rendering it difficult for viability.

Since many project failures are more related to sustainability, it is prudent for managers of international development projects to develop and promote sustainability in the implementation of international development projects particularly to be used as a case of stand-alone method in autonomous projects that bypass local institutions only to break down budgetary, organizational, and managerial structures in the aid-dependent countries (**World Bank, 1998**).

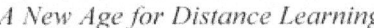
6.0 GENERAL RECOMMENDATIONS

In summary, let me argue first that there are many project management lapses in international development projects that account for project failure and that knowledge of them already exists. However, I wish to suggest and recommend the following for consideration in the management of international development projects to yield success.

- That project management problems in international development projects fall into four main categories: lack of decisive project management approach, organizational approach, managerial approach and sustainable approach.

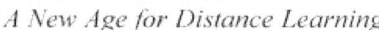

- Accordingly, I want to recommend that remedial actions (the four approaches proposed in the research) that address the four main categories of project management failure, all together, be endorsed and practiced by project managers to substantially improve international development project implementation to increase the chances for project success in developing countries.

- That if developing countries have to develop from the implementation of international development projects they have to break free and tend to accept the existence of development concepts, asserting that any country adopting good policies will escape poverty and be developed.

7.0 CONCLUSION: A NEW PERSPECTIVE

This paper explores the contribution of international project management to development in developing countries. It is based on the four basic strategies I proposed to include: The decisive project management approach which stressed that effective management can improve the chances of international development project success in developing countries; the organizational approach which focuses on the organization's abilities and capacity to resolve project management problems; the managerial approach which tends to offer useful methodologies, approaches, tools and techniques for international development projects and lastly the sustainable approach which promote the perception of sustainability in the implementation of international development projects- particularly to be used as a case of stand-alone method in autonomous projects that bypass local institutions only to break down budgetary,

organizational, and managerial structures in the aid-dependent countries.

As these approaches are not entirely specific to international project management in international development projects, it is possible to use them collectively. This paper calls for attention to be focused on these four project management approaches in the implementation of international development projects as a means increasing the chances for project success in developing countries.

This paper then proposes an agenda for action to efficiently implement international development projects and make them more effective and efficient for the billions of dollar been directed to development purposes in developing countries. In doing so, this paper encourages a move away from the prevailing single-out project management approach in international development and refocuses project management for international development on managing objectives for long-term development results, to increase the

managerial skills of implementing and supervising agencies in developing countries, and to adapt project management in these countries cultures.

Finally, though this paper aims to contribute to making international development projects succeed in developing countries. Thus, I hasten to admit that making international development projects succeed may all point to using international project management as the decisive tool in the process. Despite this unresolved debate, international developing projects in developing countries are likely to fail if the above mentioned four approaches to international project management are not adhere to.

8.0   REFERENCES

Ahsan, K., & Gunawan, I. (2010). *Analysis of cost and schedule performance of international development projects*. International Journal of Project Management, 28(1), 68-78.

European Commission. (2007). Support to sector programs: Covering the three financing modalities: Sector budget support, Pool funding and EC project procedures. Tools and Methods Series. Guidelines2

Golini, Ruggero; Landoni, Paolo. *Impact Assessment & Project Appraisal*, 2014, Vol. 32 Issue 2, p121-135, 15p; DOI: 10.1080/14615517.2014.894088

Khang, D. B., & Moe, T. L. (2008). *Success criteria and factors for international development projects: A life-cycle-based framework*. Project Management Journal, 39(1), 72-84.

World Bank. (1998). Assessing aid: What works, what doesn't and why. Oxford, England: Oxford University Press.

www.ingramcontent.com/pod-product-compliance
Lightning Source LLC
Chambersburg PA
CBHW081806170526
45167CB00008B/3346